SHAKESPEARE'S
LONDON

A GUIDE TO ELIZABETHAN LONDON

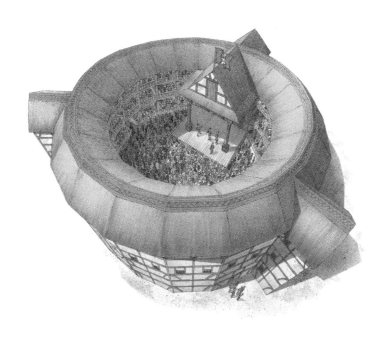

JULIE FERRIS

NEW YORK

Written and edited by   Julie Ferris
Senior Designer   Jane Tassie

Consultant   Nicholas Robins
Illustrations   Inklink Firenze
Kevin Maddison

KINGFISHER
Larousse Kingfisher Chambers Inc.
95 Madison Avenue
New York, New York 10016

First published in 2000
2 4 6 8 10 9 7 5 3 1

1TR/1199/WKT/AT(AT)/140MA

LIBRARY OF CONGRESS CATALOGING-IN-PUBLICATION DATA
Ferris, Julie.
Shakespeare's London/ by Julie Ferris. —1st ed.
p. cm.—(Sightseers)
Includes index.
Summary: In a travel guide format, presents a look at the sites and socitey that existed
in London during the time of William Shakespeare.
1. London (England)—History—16th century—Juvenile literature. 2. London
(England)—History—17th century—Juvenile literature. 3. Shakespeare, William
1564–1616—Homes and haunts—England—London—Juvenile literature. [1. London
(England)—Social life and customs—16th century. 2. London (England)—social life and
customs—17th century.] I. Title. II. Series.
DA680 .F47 2000
942.1—dc21   99–040377

ISBN 0-7534-5234-0

Printed in Hong Kong

Contents

Introducing London

It is the ideal time to visit this lively, bustling city. Queen Elizabeth has reigned over England for 31 years, and this political stability has brought economic and cultural prosperity to the country. London has grown rapidly in size and is now an international trade center. It is also a very popular destination for travelers, with plenty of sights and entertainments to choose from.

Queen Elizabeth has been nicknamed the "Virgin Queen" because she has never married. She is the daughter of Henry VIII and Anne Boleyn, and she became queen in 1558.

Sightseers' tip As well as visiting established tourist sights such as the Tower of London, St. Paul's Cathedral, and London Bridge, it is well worth spending time exploring the narrow, medieval streets with their overhanging, half-timbered houses.

England is now a Protestant country, and Queen Elizabeth is head of the Church.

Foreign visitors are not always treated well. Children sometimes shout insults at them.

The city wall runs around three sides of London. On the fourth side is the Thames River.

Elizabeth's reign has seen an increase in the amount and variety of entertainments available in London. Popular amusements include dancing, music, bearbaiting, archery, and soccer. The new theaters, located on the south bank of the Thames River, across from the city, are a major attraction for Londoners and visitors alike. Try to catch a play by the promising young playwright William Shakespeare. There are daily performances of his plays at the Globe Theatre, which opened earlier this year.

The recently built Royal Exchange is the trading and banking heart of the city. Every day it is packed with traders doing business.

Traveling around

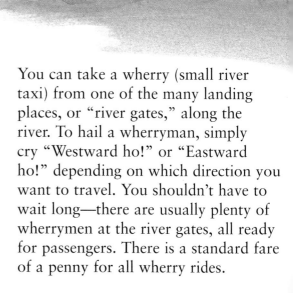

Although it is one of the largest cities in Europe, everything in London is within walking distance. However, the narrow streets and lanes are smelly and muddy and are always crowded with people, carts, and horses. It is much more pleasant, and often faster, to travel to different parts of the city by boat on the Thames River.

Sightseers' tip Wherries are light rowboats small enough to dart in and out of river traffic. The seats are comfortable and many have awnings to protect passengers from rain.

Travel on horseback if you are planning to venture out of the city. It is by far the fastest form of transportation.

You can take a wherry (small river taxi) from one of the many landing places, or "river gates," along the river. To hail a wherryman, simply cry "Westward ho!" or "Eastward ho!" depending on which direction you want to travel. You shouldn't have to wait long—there are usually plenty of wherrymen at the river gates, all ready for passengers. There is a standard fare of a penny for all wherry rides.

If traveling out of London, you can stay overnight at one of the many wayside inns.

 Traffic is becoming a problem in London and accidents are becoming more common.

Roads are in very poor condition, especially outside the city. It can take a day to travel 25 miles.

Male visitors should think twice before traveling by coach— it is considered very unmanly to ride inside a carriage.

Recently introduced from Germany, the coach has become an increasingly popular form of transportation. However, coaches do not have a suspension system, so they are uncomfortable to travel in, particularly over rough ground. At least they are covered, and will protect passengers from bad weather.

What to wear

L ondon is not the place for shrinking violets. Fashions are constantly changing and are often outrageous. Men wear doublets, breeches, stockings, and short cloaks. Women wear elaborate gowns with wide skirts and stiff corsets. Many fashion trends, such as the distinctive ruff worn around the neck, have been greatly influenced by the royal court.

If you have enough money you will be able to afford garments made of satin, velvet, and silk, and decorated with feathers and jewels. The poor, however, wear coarse, ill-fitting clothes.

Sightseers' tip The starched linen ruffs worn around the neck may be very fashionable, but they are uncomfortable and restrict movement. Many people find it difficult to eat when wearing them.

The fashion of blacking out the front teeth is handy for disguising genuinely rotten teeth.

Besides scarlet and blue, fashion colors include gooseturd green and pease-porridge yellow.

The demand for wig hair means that children out alone could get their hair chopped off!

In England, as in other European countries, there are laws dictating who can wear what. The purpose of these laws is to make people lower in rank than nobles wear plainer clothes. Traders, for example, are not allowed to wear certain expensive furs.

A pomander tied to the belt helps disguise some of the unpleasant smells around town.

You will need help getting dressed. Most garments have to be pinned, tied, or laced together.

Trimmed beards and mustaches are considered de rigueur for gentlemen. Fashionable ladies usually wear their hair up. They paint their faces with white lead and vinegar and color their lips bright red. Candle wax is smoothed onto the skin to disguise the pockmarks left by smallpox, but it tends to melt if the wearer stands too close to a fire.

As soon as they are out of baby clothes, children are dressed as young adults. Boys are dressed in the same clothes as girls until they are five years old, when they begin to wear breeches.

Food and drink

The quality and variety of food you eat during your visit to London will depend largely on your budget. If money is tight, you will have to make do with a basic diet of vegetables, bread, and the occasional meat dish. If money is no object, be prepared for lavish banquets.

Meat such as venison and pheasant is hung in a storeroom for several days to improve the taste.

The Catholic custom of eating fish on Fridays still continues in Protestant England.

Too many sweet things and a lack of milk mean bad teeth are common.

Banquets can have as many as ten courses, but don't be dismayed by the amount of food. It is the custom to eat only one or two mouthfuls of each course. Popular dishes include venison, mutton, and swan, with fruit pies and gelatin for dessert.

Although a few water pumps have been installed in the city, most people still rely on water carriers. They sell water door-to-door and often wear a towel over their clothes to keep them dry.

Sightseers' tip

Most people have two big meals a day— at midday and in the early evening. The rich wash their food down with wine, while the poor drink ale.

Forks have only recently been introduced from Italy and are not in common use. Diners are usually provided with a napkin and spoon, but guests are sometimes expected to bring their own knives. It is polite to wash your hands before and after eating— especially because you often have to eat with your fingers.

Pewter pots and plates are popular, but also very costly. Some people rent their supply of pewter by the year.

Shopping

London is a great place for shopping. Most streets are lined with stores and crowded with peddlers advertising their wares. You will, however, have to walk to different parts of the city to buy different things. For example, vintners (wine merchants) can be found in Vintry Lane, and bakers are grouped together in Bread Lane and Pudding Lane.

Why not commission a miniature portrait of yourself? It would make a great souvenir of your trip.

Storekeepers and their apprentices usually live in the same house as their business.

Booksellers in St. Paul's churchyard sell copies of the latest plays, including Shakespeare's.

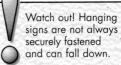
Watch out! Hanging signs are not always securely fastened and can fall down.

There are strict regulations for storekeepers. Each trade has its own guild. No one can open a store or practice a particular craft unless they have served a full apprenticeship of seven years, and paid an entrance fee to join the appropriate guild. The quality and price of goods are carefully controlled and monitored, and heavy fines are imposed on storekeepers who use false weights and measures.

Hanging signs should indicate what a store sells, but sometimes they are not changed when the store changes hands. You may, for example, see a goldsmith's store with a bookseller's sign.

Sightseers' tip

Apprentices often call out to passersby to encourage business. However, you may be subjected to rude comments from an apprentice if you examine goods without buying them.

Accommodation

Where you stay depends largely on your budget. If money is no object, you will be able to stay in a fine, half-timbered Elizabethan town house with servants to attend to your needs. If this is not in your budget, you may find yourself in a slum house, sharing a bed with several people.

At midnight, night watchmen remind people to lock their doors and douse fires.

If you're lucky enough to stay in the home of a wealthy Londoner, you will be impressed by the beautifully carved oak furniture. You should also get a good night's sleep—huge four-poster beds are a status symbol in England.

Besides having soft pillows, a mattress, and a warm coverlet, four-poster beds are hung with curtains to keep in the warmth at night.

The introduction of chimneys earlier this century put an end to smoke-filled rooms.

London has many rat-infested slums, particularly in the east end of the city.

The inns on the roads out of London are very comfortable and have an excellent reputation.

Sightseers' tip

Each floor of an Elizabethan house juts out over the floor below. There is such a small gap between the top stories of houses that they practically meet in the middle of the street.

Floors are covered with a layer of rushes. The rushes are often left unchanged for many months, so vermin, filth, and bad smells are common. Perfumers are employed by homeowners to cover up bad odors.

The master of the house can relax in a comfortable oak chair with armrests. The other members of the household have to make do with wooden stools.

The royal court has recently witnessed the introduction of a new sanitary device called the water closet. Unlike the chamber pot, this new invention uses water to flush away human waste. However, it is expensive and hasn't caught on yet.

The Globe Theatre

N o trip to London would be complete without a visit to one of the theaters on the south bank of the Thames. Although the first theater was built only 23 years ago, plays have proved extremely popular, and thousands flock to the theaters every day. Entry to a performance costs one penny. You will have to pay another penny for a seat in the gallery.

William Shakespeare is the city's most popular playwright. He is a member of the theater company based at the Globe, the Lord Chamberlain's Men.

Only men can be actors, so the female roles in plays are taken by boys.

Each theater stages about 20 plays a year. New plays have to be approved by the Master of the Revels. He reports to the Lord Chamberlain and has the power to cut lines or even ban plays if he feels they are offensive or undermine authority.

The Globe Theatre opened earlier this year. It is one of the largest in London and can hold up to 3,000 spectators. Watch out for cutpurses (thieves) who operate in the crowds during performances.

Fruit, cakes, and drinks are sold by hawkers during performances.

 Make sure you wear warm clothes—theaters are open-air.

 You may need to hire a wherry to take you across the river to the theaters.

Sightseers' tip A raised flag indicates that there will be a performance. Plays are held in the afternoon and a trumpet is blasted three times to signal the start.

Fashionable London gentlemen pay for seats on the stage itself. They arrive late deliberately and delight in interrupting performances by coughing, yawning, or making rude remarks. The rest of the audience can also be very rowdy, making the theater an exciting place to visit.

Leisure time

There is no shortage of amusements to entertain the visitor to London. You can try your hand at some popular sports such as bowling, skittles, field hockey, and soccer. If you prefer a more relaxing time, many households enjoy musical evenings where everyone sings and plays musical instruments.

Londoners enjoy playing board games such as backgammon and chess.

London taverns are famous for the lively chatter and merry wit of their patrons. But they are also the scene of frequent brawls.

Bloodthirsty sports such as bullbaiting and bearbaiting are extremely popular. Fierce dogs are set on a tethered bear or bull, and bets are made on the outcome. Londoners also enjoy watching cockfights, and gamble large sums of money on which bird will win.

Sightseers' tip

Cockfights are held in Birdcage Walk and St. Giles-in-the-Fields. The cocks fight to the death, so it's not for the squeamish.

Amusements end early in the evening because the streets get very dark and crime is common.

 There are archery shooting butts set up outside the city walls in the Moorfields.

 The Lord Mayor's Show is held every year and includes a water pageant and a land procession.

Soccer is played using a leather ball. There are few rules. Two teams from different parts of the city meet between the two areas, and the object of the game is to get the ball back to your own part of the city any way you can. It is a very rough game and players are often injured.

The authorities frown on the playing of soccer because it is a frequent cause of riots and bloodshed.

St. Paul's Cathedral

Dominating the London skyline, St. Paul's Cathedral marks the center of the city, and is a must for sightseers. The huge, gothic cathedral is very much a part of city life. Londoners go there not only to worship and listen to sermons, but also to do business and gossip.

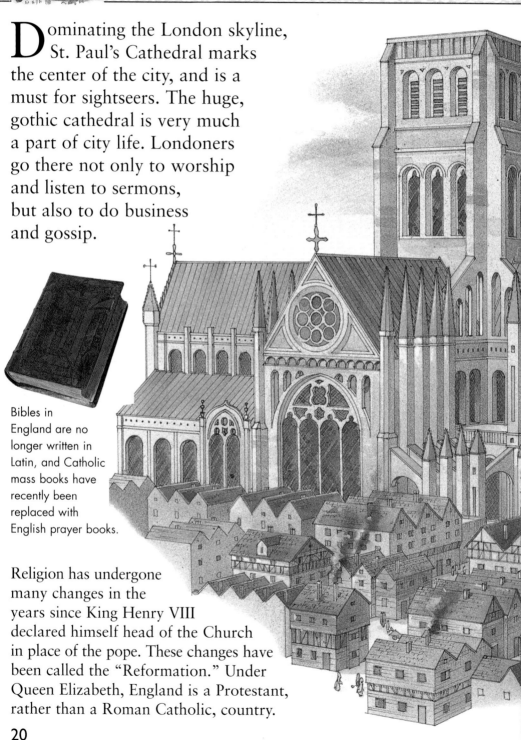

Bibles in England are no longer written in Latin, and Catholic mass books have recently been replaced with English prayer books.

Religion has undergone many changes in the years since King Henry VIII declared himself head of the Church in place of the pope. These changes have been called the "Reformation." Under Queen Elizabeth, England is a Protestant, rather than a Roman Catholic, country.

There are laws requiring attendance at church on Sundays, but fines are rarely imposed.

Many tourists have left their mark by carving messages in St. Paul's soft lead roof.

For a small price, the bellman allows children to climb the bell tower and drop things from the top.

If you are expecting the interior of St. Paul's to be a peaceful, solemn place, get ready for a surprise. Londoners gather in the cathedral daily to exchange news and chat, show off new clothes, meet friends, do business, and hire servants. The aisles have even been used as a shortcut when driving cattle to market.

Sightseers' tip

The cathedral's central aisle is known as "Paul's Walk." Every morning, it is crowded with people from all parts of London society, including cutpurses—so watch your valuables.

Paul's Cross is an open-air pulpit in the cathedral's grounds. Sermons are preached here every Sunday.

St. Paul's Cathedral originally had a 526-foot high steeple, but this burned down when it was struck by lightning in 1561.

The Tower of London

In the east of the city is the famous Tower of London. It has a long and bloody history and is definitely worth a visit. As well as being a royal palace, the Tower is a prison and it is the only place in England where coins are minted. It is also home to the royal armory, the crown jewels, and an animal menagerie.

Sightseers' tip

The Tower of London is very popular with sightseers. Visitors wishing to see all its attractions should be prepared to tip officials generously.

The huge body armor of Henry VIII (Queen Elizabeth's father) is part of the impressive royal armory held at the Tower.

Be careful not to offend or insult the queen during your stay, or you could enter the Tower as a prisoner through Traitor's Gate! Although high-ranking prisoners live in comfort with their own servants, most people imprisoned in the Tower endure terrible, dank conditions, suffer cruel tortures, and face eventual execution.

Two of Henry VIII's six wives were beheaded at the Tower, and Queen Elizabeth was once imprisoned here.

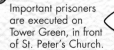
Important prisoners are executed on Tower Green, in front of St. Peter's Church.

The royal armory was established by Henry VIII. It contains all the latest weapons and armor.

The fierce lions are the most popular animals in the menagerie. Wooden lattices have been built to protect visitors.

The biggest draw to the Tower is the collection of wild animals in the royal menagerie. The tiger, wolf, porcupine, and the two lions kept in the Tower are not native to England, and are therefore a great curiosity for Londoners and visitors alike.

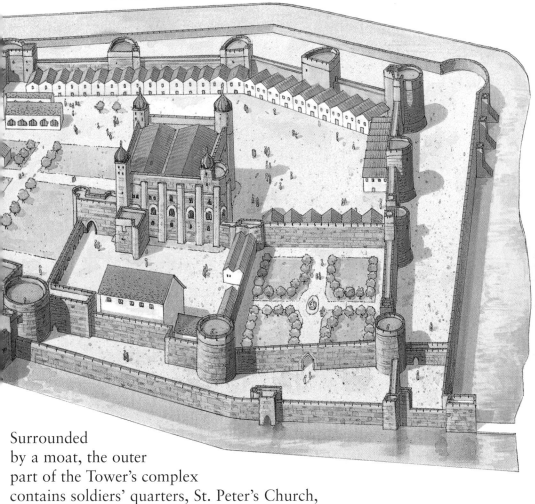

Surrounded by a moat, the outer part of the Tower's complex contains soldiers' quarters, St. Peter's Church, and gardens. Special permission is needed to enter the inner courtyard and the 11th-century White Tower.

London Bridge

The world-famous London Bridge is the only bridge across the Thames River and is a "must-see" for visitors. Built on 20 stone arches, it is so crowded with stores, chapels, and houses that it looks more like a street than a bridge.

Sightseers' tip There is a wide variety of stores on London Bridge, but it is especially noted for the manufacture and retail of dress pins. There are usually crowds of people around the bridge's narrow stands.

The road through the bridge is scarcely wider than a single cart and collisions happen frequently. The buildings overhang the road so much that it is always gloomy, even during the day.

A victim of the Reformation, St. Thomas's Chapel at the center of the bridge is now a grocery store.

Stores are crammed so tightly that only a 12-foot wide passage is left for traffic.

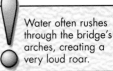
Water often rushes through the bridge's arches, creating a very loud roar.

The bridge slows down the river current, causing the Thames to freeze in cold weather. Frost fairs, with sports and games, are sometimes organized on the ice.

The bridge's massive piers act a little like a dam, holding the water back and causing it to rush through the arches, which makes it very dangerous to travel under the bridge by boat—a little like shooting the rapids. The phenomenon has even given rise to a local proverb: "London Bridge was made for wise men to walk over and fools to go under."

Londoners flock to public executions and are used to seeing bloody heads displayed on poles.

At either end of London Bridge stand imposing gate towers. The squeamish are advised not to look up when approaching the gate at the southern end. Impaled on poles over the tower are the shriveled heads of those executed for high treason.

25

The royal court

Now that Queen Elizabeth is in her sixties, the royal court is not as lively as it once was. However, if you manage to get an invitation you will be able to see the opulent lifestyle of the queen and her rich and powerful courtiers firsthand.

Hunting is a very popular royal sport. Queen Elizabeth owns several deer parks where she goes stag hunting with her courtiers and important foreign visitors.

The court moves between several royal residences, including the palaces of Greenwich (pictured above), Richmond, Hampton Court, and Nonsuch.

In summer, the royal court travels around the country, staying at the homes of nobles.

When the court moves to a new palace, furniture, tapestries, and treasures are taken with them.

If you wish to attend court and see the queen you will need a pass from the Lord Chamberlain.

Make sure you visit Westminster Abbey, the magnificent medieval church to the west of London. As well as containing many royal tombs, it also houses the coronation chair on which kings and queens are crowned.

The royal court is the center of government in England. Queen Elizabeth is a very skillful ruler and has surrounded herself with faithful admirers. She uses social occasions to discuss important matters with her advisers or foreign visitors.

Sightseers' tip

In the evenings, the royal court enjoys dancing. The most popular dance is called the volta. Men and women dance together. The man clasps the woman around the waist and lifts her into the air.

27

Survival guide

During Elizabeth's long reign, England has remained a peaceful and prosperous country. London has grown rapidly, and visitors will find it a very lively and exciting city. However, the increase in population means that outbreaks of plague and disease are common, and crime is widespread.

Administration

Queen Elizabeth, with advice from her officials, decides foreign policy and internal legislation. If she needs to raise taxes or pass new laws she calls a parliament, although during her long reign she has called very few. The city of London is governed by a lord mayor and aldermen, who meet regularly at the Guildhall. The aldermen are usually powerful merchants and are elected from London's 26 wards. One of them is chosen to be lord mayor.

Prices have risen throughout Elizabeth's reign. Currency includes gold sovereigns (one pound), angels (ten shillings), and silver crowns (five shillings).

Health

The streets of London are filthy and there are rats and other vermin everywhere. Illness and diseases such as smallpox, cholera, and measles are also very common.

No one yet knows what causes the frequent outbreaks of bubonic plague, although many think it is a divine punishment from God. Sneezing is an early symptom of the plague, and death usually follows within five days. To ward off the disease, doctors recommend that you carry a garland of herbs.

Most people die young. Only one out of ten people reaches the age of 40.

There is a large number of beggars. Some pretend to be injured so people will give them more money.

Town criers announce forthcoming events, new laws, and plague warnings.

Law and order

Although there is no paid police force, criminals who are caught face severe punishments. Penalties for petty crimes include a spell in the pillory, stocks, or "ducking stool." You could also have your face branded, your ears clipped, or your nose slit.

While common people are hanged, nobles face the block and ax. However, the ax is rarely sharp enough to sever the head in one stroke.

Those accused of witchcraft are plunged into water on a ducking stool. If they drown they are innocent, but if they survive they are declared witches and are executed. Ducking stools are also used to punish nagging wives who refuse to obey their husbands. Theft, riot, treason, and murder are punishable by death.

People who commit minor crimes face the humiliation of a spell in the pillory or stocks. Criminals are incarcerated in a public place and passersby throw rotten food at them.

29

❓ Souvenir quiz

Take your time exploring Shakespeare's London. It is a fascinating city with a lot to see and experience. Before you leave, test your knowledge with this fun quiz. You will find the answers on page 32.

1. Coins are minted in only one place in England. Where is it?

a) The Royal Exchange— the trading and banking heart of the city.

b) The Tower of London—where the royal armory and the crown jewels are kept.

c) The Guildhall—where the lord mayor and aldermen meet.

2. Stores and businesses in London are strictly regulated. What do you have to do before you can open a store or practice a craft?

a) Serve a seven-year apprenticeship and pay a fee to join the appropriate guild.

b) Write to the queen asking for royal permission.

c) Pay the lord mayor five gold sovereigns.

3. Why should you avoid standing below hanging street signs?

a) They are not always securely fastened and can sometimes fall down.

b) Superstitious Londoners believe it will give you seven years' bad luck.

c) Storekeepers do not like people loitering outside their shops.

4. Why do the authorities frown upon the playing of soccer?

a) They only sanction board games such as chess.

b) Leisure time should be used for archery practice.

c) It is a frequent cause of riots and bloodshed.

5. Punishments in Elizabethan London are very severe. How are nagging wives who refuse to obey their husbands punished?

a) Their ears are clipped and their faces branded with a hot iron.

b) They are executed.

c) They are put on a "ducking stool" and plunged into water.

6. What is a wherry?

a) A small boat used as a river taxi.

b) One of London Bridge's 20 stone arches.

c) A hawker who sells fruit during theater performances.

7. Londoners enjoy bloodthirsty sports. What happens in bearbaiting?

a) Bears are hunted in the woods outside the city.

b) Fierce dogs are set on a tethered bear.

c) Bears are chased through the streets by children.

8. St. Paul's central aisle is usually crowded with people chatting and doing business. What is its nickname?

a) It is known as Cathedral Close.

b) It is called Paul's Progress.

c) It is known as Paul's Walk.

9. Why do Londoners consider it fashionable to blacken their front teeth?

a) It contrasts well with their painted white faces.

b) Because the queen has no front teeth.

c) It disguises genuinely rotten teeth.

10. At which theater is William Shakespeare an actor and a playwright?

a) The Globe.

b) The Swan.

c) The Rose.

Index

Acknowledgments

The consultant
Nicholas Robins works at Shakespeare's Globe Theatre in London and is the editor of its magazine, *Around the Globe.*

Inklink Firenze illustrators
Simone Boni, Alessandro Rabatti, Lorenzo Pieri, Luigi Critone, Lucia Mattioli, Francisco Petracchi, Theo Caneschi

Additional illustrations
Vanessa Card, Jason Lewis, Nicki Palin

Picture Research Manager
Jane Lambert

Picture credits
b = bottom, c = center, l = left, r = right, t = top

p.4 tr Burghley House Collection, Lincolnshire, U.K./ Bridgeman Art Library, London/New York; p.5 cr O'Shea Gallery, London/Bridgeman Art Library, London/New York; p.9 tl In the collection of the Duke of Buccleuch & Queensberry, KT, cr Asprey & Co., London/Bridgeman Art Library, London/ New York, br Burghley House Collection, Lincolnshire/ Bridgeman Art Library, London/New York; p.11 br Museum of London Archaeological Service; p.12 tl Christies Images; p.16 tl AKG London; p.18 tr Mary Rose Trust; p.20 cl Dean and Chapter of Westminster; p.22 tl The Board of Trustees of the Armouries, (II.8); p.25 tl Fulgoni Photography; p.26 bl National Trust Photographic Library; p.27 tr Courtesy of the Dean and Chapter of Westminster/ Angelo Hornak; p.28 bl ET Archive/British Museum.

Every effort has been made to trace the copyright holders of the photographs. The publishers apologize for any inconvenience caused.

Souvenir quiz answers

1 = b) 2 = a) 3 = a) 4 = c) 5 = c) 6 = a) 7 = b) 8 = c) 9 = c) 10 = a)

The setting for this Sightseers guide is 1599.